DOCTOR, WHEN YOU'RE SICK YOU'RE NOT WELL

Forty Years of Outpatient Humour from Twillingate Hospital, Newfoundland

DOCTOR, WHEN YOU'RE SICK YOU'RE NOT WELL

Forty Years of Outpatient Humour from Twillingate Hospital, Newfoundland

Gary L. Saunders

BREAKWATER

BREAKWATER
100 Water St.
P.O. Box 2188
St. John's, NF
A1E 6E6

Front Cover Illustration: "Dr John McKee Olds sounding a young patient" by
Gary L. Saunders
Back Cover Photo: Gary L. Saunders
Design and Production: Lori R. O'Brien
Illustrations: Gary L. Saunders

Canadian Cataloguing in Publication Data

Saunders, Gary L.

Doctor, When You're Sick You're Not Well: Forty
Years of Outpatient Humour from Twillingate
Hospital, Newfoundland

ISBN 1-55081-142-8

1. Hospitals — Outpatient services — Newfoundland —
Humour.   2. Medicine — Newfoundland — Humour.
3. Notre Dame Bay Memorial Hospital — Humour.
4. English Language — Dialects — Newfoundland.
5. Olds, John McKee, 1906-1985. I. Saunders, Gary L. II.
Olds, John McKee, 1906-1985.

R705.D63 1998   610'.9718   C98-901176-3

Printed in Canada

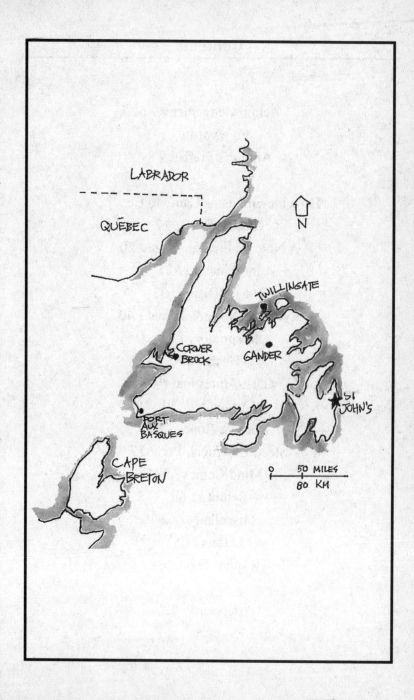

Contents

**To all the aides and nurses
who made the wheels go round**

Acknowledgements

B ut for the foresight of Angela Jenkins, long-time librarian at Notre Dame Bay Memorial Hospital, these sayings might have been lost. It was she found and saved them, and she who told me about them.

For helpful comments on the manuscript I especially thank my spouse Beth, Dr John Sheldon, Lorna and Gord Stuckless, and Eric Facey. I also owe a debt to the many physicians and writers, living or dead, whose words are sprinkled through the text. I found most of them in Dr Robert Coope's wonderful collection entitled *The Quiet Art* (E. & S. Livingstone Ltd of Britain, 1952.) In one of life's lovely convergences, this book was given to me in 1991 by a 1951 summer student of Dr Olds's, namely Dr Jim Pittman, later Dean of the University of Alabama School of Medicine.

Of course the real credit belongs to John McKee Olds, M. D., for taking time during his hectic life to save these gems of Newfoundland English.

Foreword

Angela Jenkins

I doubt very much that health care in our part of rural Newfoundland would have been what it was and what it is today if it were not for the dedication and selflessness of the late Dr John Olds. I think Charles Dickens did a good job of describing Dr Olds in this passage from *The Mystery of Edwin Drood:*

> He was simply and staunchly true to his duty alike
> in the large case and in the small. So all true souls are.
> So every true soul ever was, ever is, and ever will be.
> There is nothing little to the really great in spirit.

The ability to appreciate the comic absurdities present in people and situations is commonly known as having a sense of humour. Anyone who ever worked with Dr Olds or was a patient of his knew him to be anything but jocular. You can usually tell if someone has a sense of humour—but not always. You can actually work with a person for years and suddenly realize he has another side, an aspect of his personality you never thought existed.

This was my experience with Dr Olds.

— From an address to health care workers on the 25th anniversary of the Newfoundland Hospital and Nursing Home Association.

Author's Preface

Laughter is the best medicine.
— Anonymous

When I went to Twillingate in October 1989 to interview people for a book on Dr Olds, the first person I met was Edwin Hamlyn of nearby Crow Head. Mr Hamlyn was a burly carpenter who lived across the road from my rented bungalow; in fact he had built it. I had hardly unpacked when he was inviting me over for "a cup o' tay."

During tea, he spoke of the hard life Twillingaters had endured years ago, toiling at the fish "from daylight to star dark." When I remarked how well the hill to the north sheltered his place he said, "Aye, that it do," but allowed that "the sou'wester is our spitiest wind."

To my untrained ear, he spoke with the West Country accents of my Gander Bay childhood. In fact these Hamlyns hailed from Yorkshire in the north of England. Still, his speech recalled the melodious words of Uncle Hezekiah, of Aunt Carrie, of Uncle Ben and all the rest. That night I slept better than I had in months.

In the busy weeks of interviewing that followed, several people alluded to a mysterious "book of patients' sayings." I never expected to see this book, but asked Angela Jenkins about it anyway. Yes, she said, there was such a thing. Or rather, a number of scribblers and notebooks. And she had found and saved two of them.

When she lent them to me, I felt like an anthropologist stumbling on a new Beothuk wordlist. Every page sparkled with expected turns of speech, with wordplay, with odd logic—in short, with authentic Newfoundland humour.

Angela also gave me a copy of a speech she had given years before. She had called it "Doctor, When You're Sick, You're Not Well: A Comical Side to Health Care." A perfect title for my book.

". . . every invalid is really a special case, a unique example."
—H. F. Amiel

The two surviving notebooks span thirty-nine years: from 1943—Olds's darkest year—to 1982, three years before he died. There is a gap in the fifties, when he was ill from overwork and alcohol. World War II had stolen all his doctors and nurses one by one, leaving him virtually alone between 1943 and 1945. In 1943 three more calamities befell him: a night fire demolished the Hospital's third floor, his wife Betty sickened with chronic kidney disease and his father died.

John slogged on, running this 90-bed hospital, coping with wartime shortages, performing several operations a day, battling a tuberculosis epidemic. He was on duty seven days a week, at all hours. He took to drinking—not enough to compromise his work, just enough to dull the pain. He developed some sort of lung lesion. When he began to cough up blood, his directors shipped him to a United States sanatorium. He returned healthier, but soon went back on the bottle. By the time Betty died in 1954, he was a physical and mental wreck. Only an enforced medical leave saved him and his sanity. Soon he was carrying almost as heavy a load as before.

Dr Fred Woodruff, who worked at the hospital from 1963 to 1988, recalled in 1990 how the notebooks were revived:

> Dr Olds was never unkind to his patients; he used to love to laugh with them. He'd often come out of the examining room chuckling and say: "What do you think of this one?" These were always short things—one-liners, you might say.
>
> We'd been discussing the wealth of really first-class stories some of those old people carried around in their heads. So I said to him one day: "Why don't you write these things down?"
>
> "No, my son; not worth the bother." But Dr Olds finally agreed that if I got him a book, he'd write some of them in.

John Olds kept his word. Some of the sayings and witticisms came from ward rounds, some from house calls and a few from the OR. Since, however, most came from Outpatients, he named them "OPDisms." The man was too busy to be systematic about it, and many sayings were lost. But he found it therapeutic.

Naturally, I wove a few OPDisms into *Doctor Olds of Twillingate*. After it came out in 1994, I toyed with publishing the rest. It seemed a shame to hoard such treasures. The thing that held me back was a fear of offending former patients. After all, these OPDisms came out of pain and fear—and, in the case of TB, of shame as well. No laughing matter.

Besides, what did I know of pain? I'd never even been in a hospital overnight. That changed in 1995. And during my bouts with scalpel and catheter and cystoscope and with filiform followers and the mighty Fleet and barium enemas, I came to appreciate the pathos in such exchanges as this:

Doctor: "Skipper, how's your water since you had your operation?"

Patient: "Well, Doctor, some mornings I can piss over a five-barred gate—and other mornings I can't get it clear o' me gaiters!"

Perhaps, I thought, these OPDisms could help other people too.

How the OPDisms Came to Be

The old Notre Dame Bay Memorial Hospital,
Twilingate, Newfoundland, 1924-1981

Take thousands of ordinary people from the west of
England and the east of Ireland, plant them piecemeal on a
subarctic island far across the Western Sea, leave them there for
two or three centuries to toil for cod and seals and fur with only
one Book, and what will you get? Certainly you'll get a tough
and kindly folk who take little for granted and nothing, not even
Death, very seriously. You'll also get a people whose English
shines with metaphor and simile, whose supple dialect can
express with economy and vigour the bold rant of anger, the
deep chill of fear, the randy yen of lust, the nish pain of grief.

Now should any of these people come down with a real or
fancied illness, and find themselves closeted in the dreaded
hospital with the dreaded doctor, they are apt to forget their
accustomed reserve and talk as they would down stage or out in
boat.

And should the doctor happen to be John McKee Olds, a Connecticut Yankee who came to Twillingate as a young medical student in 1932 against the wishes of his genteel kith and kin, he will keep a straight face. Later, in the privacy of his office, he may allow himself a chuckle, even a guffaw. And he may, with half a notion of making a collection, scribble the latest *bon mot* on a prescription pad or a cigarette pack. Later he may buy a scribbler and copy them in.

That's exactly what happened at Notre Dame Bay Memorial Hospital. Patients came from the whole Bay, from Baie Verte in the west to Cape Freels in the east, from Corner Brook and beyond. Once registered, they waited to see The Doctor, meaning preferably John Olds, M. D., F. A. C. S., Chief of Surgery and longtime Hospital Superintendent.

The one big fear most patients had was that they would have to stay in hospital. To them, brought up hearing medical horror stories from their grandparents—stories which were mostly true—it seemed a death sentence.

One day on a house call Olds overheard a fisherman remark, "Oh, I knows that feller Leo; he's the one was all cut to pieces up in Twillingate."

"Dear Dr Olds," wrote a former patient, "I been to your hospital several times, but I'm not dead yet!"

Understandably then, to the first-time visitor to Twillingate Hospital the examining room was a perilous place, part confession box, part torture chamber. Outside in the waiting room, they were suffering but fairly safe. Inside this room, they were thrust into sudden intimacy with a stranger.

Ten to one the doctor would be male. For a female patient this was bad enough, but this particular male asked you probing questions, personal questions, questions that demanded honest answers because your future health rode on the outcome. All the while, he would be peering into your eyes, probing your ears and throat, tapping your rib cage, listening fore and aft with his stethoscope while you inhaled, exhaled, coughed, or held your breath on command, and perhaps feeling for things amiss in neck or abdomen, breasts—or more private places. It was scandalous when you came to think on it.

"[She] wondered why people should be so fond of the company of their physician till she recollected that he was the only person with whom one dared to talk continually of oneself, without interruption, contradiction or censure."

— Sir Robert Hutchinson

The medical staff treated out-of-town patients right away if possible. They lanced angry boils, pulled numberless rotten teeth and splinters, amputated seal fingers as big as blood-puddings. They sutured cuts, relieved constipation, diarrhea and hemorrhoids, dealt with blocked tear ducts and swollen lymph glands. They tended fretful babies, deaf-mute children, youths not right in the head, grandmothers with ingrown toenails. They even fixed ailing cats and cows. In the 1930s, when the Hospital grew much of its own meat, milk, butter, eggs and vegetables, Dr Olds routinely castrated the farm's hogs. Once or twice he operated on an injured horse. He even snipped two extra legs off a hen.

People too ill to be out-patients became in-patients. In those days, Dr Olds and his team performed everything but heart and brain surgery. Besides delivering countless babies, they sutured arms and legs sliced by axes and saws or torn by winches. They repaired bones broken by falling trees. They collapsed lungs honeycombed by TB. Children were brought to them scorched by fire or scalded in bark pots or ravaged by Gillett's lye, and most of them they nursed back to health.

"Every patient, he said, provided two questions—firstly what can be learnt from him and secondly what can be done for him."

—Harvey Cushing

When Olds wasn't in the OR, he spent most of his days and many of his nights talking with patients, listening to their pains and fears. When he first began to collect OPDisms, co-workers wondered what he was up to. When they found out, some became his collaborators. He always insisted on omitting patients' names.

How many sayings he recorded over the years is impossible now to tell. The two notebooks contain about two hundred. These and many more were told and retold within the hospital walls, where they helped to calm jittery OR nerves and to ease the daily stress of battling disease. Over time, the sayings took on a patina like that of favourite pebbles. But when the Old Man retired in 1976, they began to gather dust.

"The most important difference between a good and an indifferent clinician lies in the amount of attention paid to the story of a patient."

—Sir Farquhar Buzzard

Olds As Hero

Fortunately, most OPD visitors were soon mended and put on the next boat home. Others might stay a week, a month, a year. Once cured, they were forever grateful. They praised the Hospital and its doctors, they extolled the virtues of nurses, orderlies and aides. Above all they praised Dr Olds.

Perhaps no one admired John more than his old friend Captain Peter Troake, who died in 1997. In June of 1947 Captain Troake was rushed from his schooner to OPD with his left foot dangling by a flap of skin. A spinning engine shaft had snagged his pant leg on his way to fish the Labrador Sea. Eleven months later, he walked out of that hospital on his own two legs using only a cane. When Olds teasingly asked him who he thanked for his foot, Peter solemnly replied, "Sir, I thanks you and the Lord. And Doc, if you was to tell me, 'Pete, I got to take your head off and slew it round and you can walk backwards,' I'd say, 'Sir, you do it.'"

"'I will cause the new skin to grow and heal your wounds,'
saith the Lord. . . ."
— Jeremiah 30:17

17

One day Dr Olds's long-time secretary Mayme Hewlett was talking with an old lady who had recently undergone a very serious operation in Twillingate. "Oh yes maid," she said, "I was cut here, cut there, cut everywhere!"

"And were you nervous beforehand?" asked Mayme.

"Nervous, my dear?" cried the woman. "Why, when Dr Olds told me he was going to take care of me, I felt just as safe as if I was in God's pocket!"

Such was their faith. So loyal were some patients that they would apologize for even thinking of seeing another doctor. "I had my mind packed to go to Grand Falls," said one as he was being admitted to Notre Dame Bay Memorial, "but it didn't seem right so I came here."

They wrote him from all over the Bay to express that loyalty. A woman from Bay Verte sent this Christmas greeting: "I wish DR. OLDS a Merry Christmas and a Happy New Year and live to be a million years of age. With all good health to carry on his good works."

If he made a minor mistake, they forgave him. A woman he had operated on came in complaining of pain when she bent over. The X-ray showed a pair of tweezers in her abdomen. Said Olds, "I left those tweezers in there. You have two choices: you can tell the world, or you can let me take 'em out. The operation will take about five minutes." She chose the operation.

"A man's body and his mind. . . are exactly like a jerkin and a jerkin's lining; rumple the one, you rumple the other."

— Laurence Stern
Tristram Shandy

Many doctors and nurses remarked on the man's extraordinary empathy with patients. He had been head physician in Twillingate since 1934, had travelled all over Notre Dame Bay in all weathers and seasons. Thousands knew him and looked on him as their family doctor. Many, arriving at Outpatients, would consent to see no other.

"Oh no," said a Twillingate woman in her seventies, "the minute you knew that Dr Olds was around, well, you'd have to see him. If you went there and got someone else to examine you, you didn't have an easy mind. He forgot more than those doctors will ever know. I wouldn't go up there now for an operation; you couldn't pay me enough money. . . there wouldn't be enough anesthetic in the Hospital for to put me to sleep."

Dr Fred Woodruff described him as almost a faith healer.

"In a way, he practised a bit of voodoo. I'd go over to Outpatients and he'd be there. And a fellow would come in and say, 'Dr Olds, 'tis all in me knee.' And Olds would put the stethoscope on the man's knee, and he'd listen.

"'You're OK,' he'd say.

"'Thank you, Dr Hose.'

"Or another would say, ''Tis all in me 'ead, Doctor.' Olds might have been waiting, looking at a *Time* magazine or something. And he'd put his stethoscope to the fella's head and listen for a minute and close his eyes and he'd say, 'Skipper, I've got just the pill for you! You'll be okay.'

"'Thank you, Dr Holds.'

"They treated him with such awe."

"[A doctor's] greatest skill perhaps. . . lies in the infusing of hope, and inducing some composure and tranquillity of mind before they enter upon the other operations of their art."

— Sir William Temple
Of Health and Long Life

A Note on the Language

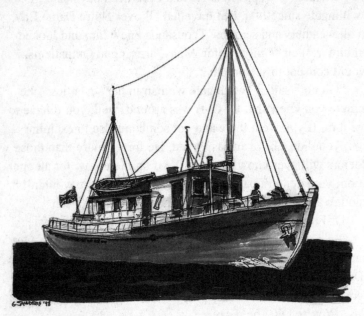

The hospital boat, the *Bonnie Nell II,* around 1960

For most doctors and medical students fresh from Away, outport speech must have sounded at best archaic and at worst uncouth. It grated on their educated ears the way American speech is said to grate on English ears.

To Dr Olds, however, it sounded broad and soft and musical, oddly familiar, oddly right. In fact, Newfoundland outport English has more in common with early American dialects than with Standard English. Both are branches of the same great language tree, that ancient hybrid of Celtic and Latin and Viking and Norman French. But whereas in England the mother tongue rapidly evolved toward what we call Oxford English, overseas it kept much of its Elizabethan lilt. American colonists, like their Newfoundland counterparts, came ashore saying *athwart* for across and *'bide* (abide) for stay, *harse* for horse and *tay* for tea. And, cut off from the Old Country by a great ocean, they went on speaking that way long after such pronunciations and expressions had vanished from Standard English. And they kept creating new words to express the realities of a new world.

Newfoundland English stayed purer still. Planted on saw-toothed capes and far up foggy tickles, hiding in chimney-corner coves to avoid unfriendly eyes, the Elizabethan rose became a bakeapple blossom. It was hardy, spare, lovely—in short, a dialect as respectable as any other.

This dialect was fresh and direct and also full of new words and quaint expressions. Like the Cockney Aussies with their *tucker bag* (knapsack) and *billabong* (pond), Newfoundlanders coined such words and phrases as *angashore* (one who shirks the sea), *tuckamore* (clump of stunted trees) and *water haul* (empty net). They even preserved one of the very few surviving Cornish Gaelic words, namely *emmet* (small ant).

Said Dr George M. Story, author of the definitive *Dictionary of Newfoundland English*, "[The result was] an unusual kind of intensification of the culture, reinforced by three centuries of successive immigration [that] virtually stopped in the mid-19th century."*

So when some rough and windburnt fisherman confronted Dr. Olds with, "Doctor, I got a maid 'ere and I wants you to see to she," he was delighted. If he asked a boy how old he was and the boy replied, "I be ten, Zir, February gone," he felt as though he had stepped into the world of Thomas Hardy; it was like talking to Shakespeare himself.

Then there was the odd arithmetic, the offbeat logic. A man, asked about his previous medication, replied, "I took a six

* *Birmingham News*, Sept. 21, 1983

weeks treatment for a couple of months." A woman, asked about the frequency of her periods, said, "Well, Sir, last month I had them three times and bled eleven days at a time."

Robert Ecke, a young American M. D. who worked with Olds in the thirties and forties, proved as fond of outport speech as he. It was like learning a new language. Mused Ecke in his journal for April 7, 1941: "The name of what I woke up with today is a bit of 'hagrod.' I suppose *hagride* is the correct word. You also hear 'sove' for 'saved' and 'scrope' for 'scraped'. . . ."

It was Dr Ecke, returning from a house call, who recorded the following mother-son exchange concerning Piercey, an otherwise healthy boy who had just been diagnosed with appendicitis:

Clemmy: "Do 'e want to go to the 'ospital and get hoperated on, or will 'e bide 'ome an' die?"
Piercey: "I'll go 'long wi' the doctor."

This was unusual; most opted to stay home and take their chances. In any case, it amazed Ecke that parents allowed young children a say in such matters. "Everything is attributed, calmly and with finality, to the 'Will of God,'" he concluded.

Something else that tickled Olds and Ecke was the way outport people mis-pronounced the two doctors' names. The most common variants were "Holds" and "Hackie." One time Olds set out to list them all; he gave up after eight or ten.

From the outset, the two young Americans tried to speak Outportese. John had a habit of mumbling ("'e can mumble better than anyone else I know," griped a student), yet he learned to do passable imitations of everything from Musgrave Harbour's broad West Country accent to Tilting's lilting Irish.

This went far to put his patients at ease.

He expected his family to speak Outportese too. One day, when young David was talking about a horse he admired, his father corrected him: "Don't say *horse*, son; say *harse*; round 'ere 'tis *harse*."

When it came to pithy language and witty rejoinders, Olds was no slouch himself. A slight man physically, by nature gentle and courteous—even shy—he cultivated a surly exterior. He cussed a lot and liked to intimidate the timid and pompous. Certain nurses scampered like mice when he appeared. Many a colleague felt the lash of his tongue. But with his patients he was remarkably tolerant.

Once, on ward rounds, he came upon a patient trying to eat a banana, peel and all. "Christ, man," he growled, "even the monkeys have enough sense to peel 'em first!" Likely it was the first banana the man had ever seen. Dr Olds peeled it for him anyway.

There was one exasperating young man in OPD who answered every question with "Whaaa. . . ?" After two or three such exchanges, Olds moved on to the next patient, and the next, and the next. Then, obviously still thinking about the monosyllabic one, and satisfied the patient wasn't deaf, he turned to the nurse, jerked his head toward him and growled, "Give that Rhodes scholar some Tylenol."

When a pregnant teen-ager complained of a fluttery feeling "like a butterfly" in her lower abdomen, he asked,

"Did you feel it flutter in?"

"No, Doctor. . . what do you mean?"

"Well, you'll damn well feel it flutter out!" He had seen innocent faces like hers so many times before.

One night he caught a male patient poking around the pharmacy, perhaps after alcohol. "What in hell are you doing out of bed?" he roared.

"Oh Doctor," said the startled man, clasping his stomach, "I got this terrible gas. . . ."

"Gas?" said Olds. "What kind of gas? Propane gas? Butane gas?"

"Ah—no-pain gas, Doctor." With that the offender scuttled back to the men's ward.

Though Olds's bark was worse than his bite, few knew it. While he lived, parents used his name to bring unruly children into line. Even after his death in 1985, the reputation lived on.

A Memorial University medical student who had done a practicum in Twillingate told me how, while boarding with a couple in nearby Moretons Harbour, the subject of Dr Olds's surliness came up. They were sitting at the kitchen table looking at the harbour when the woman said, "You know, they never buried him. . . . No, they sprinkled his ashes off Burnt Island Tickle. Mark my words—one of these days Dr Holds is gonna drive ashore!"

The Old Man would have liked that. I can see him reaching for notebook and pencil. For he did want his OPDisms preserved. Unlike butterflies, however, they can't be pinned under glass to look at now and then. The best way to preserve them is to set them free.

— Gary L. Saunders
Old Barns, Nova Scotia
June 1998

Introduction

Robert Skidmore Ecke, M. D.

I worked at Notre Dame Bay Memorial Hospital in Twillingate, Newfoundland as a summer student in 1934, and full-time from 1937 to 1942 and again in 1947 and 1948. From my first day in the hospital I was struck by outport speech. The place where I heard it the most was in the Outpatient Department, where we met and examined patients every afternoon and sometimes all day.

During those years I kept a journal:

> *Probably some of the more recently recruited aides or maids would stand and stare at me if I asked one of them to rush down to the "Outpatient Department" on an errand. [But] anybody would know where I meant if I said the "O. P. D." That's a standard term and every hospital in the U. S. uses it. One doesn't have time to use long words.*

> *I sometimes wonder what impression a more rural patient gets when he comes to the OPD for the first time. He climbs the ten concrete steps to the front door in the centre of the face of the hospital. He hauls the*

door open, grunting *against the force of the wind right off the harbour and it slams behind him with a crash that four or five times a year breaks the glass. Also as he opens the door, every other door inside the hospital swings in sympathy with the drafts. As he stands in the small square lobby, he is slightly dazed by the change in temperature and momentarily blinded by the impact of the comparative dimness after the keen glare of sky or snow.*

When his or her eyes settle down it will be clear that he is not the next patient to be seen. The lobby will have four or five people in it, the overflow from the bare-benched waiting room on the left. That space will be filled by a dozen patient citizens in their sea-going gear, with their bundles and coats and children all waiting for Bessie to invite them in through the other door to see the doctor. In an hour perhaps, it will be his turn. Meanwhile he will have inspected the plaque which describes the hospital as a memorial to the men of Notre Dame Bay who fought in World War I. Over the plaque is a small wreath, faded since its presentation last Armistice Day. Between the windows is a framed certificate wherein the College of Surgeons allows as how they consider this a reasonably good hospital. He may or may not be impressed thereby. Before he can rightly make up his mind, he is whisked by Bessie into the inner sanctum.

Here there may be something resembling confusion. The long narrow hall ends in a largish emergency room. Off the left of the hall are three examining cubicles. Doctors hustle about. Bessie is everywhere. A patient disconsolately waits in one corner for a laboratory or X-ray report. Through an inadequate screen a figure may be visible stretched on the operating table for the sewing of a laceration or the removal of a wen. From the other corner may come the vocal indications incident to the removal of a tooth. These sounds vary in sanguinity according to the skill of the operator and the emotional setup of the donor. The latter is by far the greater factor and the gamut is wide.

Bessie, an aide who has all her training right here, is the breath of the OPD. She makes the wheels go round. The OPD without her is an unlighted lamp, an unmade bed, home without a mother. She is young, not very tall and just this side of plump. She is rosy of countenance and spirit. She is wise and full of local lore, her knowledge of the people and their stories is almost alarming. On a quiet day she will espy a patient coming up the hospital lane. Before the door bell rings, Bessie will have given you a thumbnail sketch that would do credit to the dictionary of biography with a diagnosis and outline of treatment thrown in for good measure.

To do her justice, she does blush and sort of look at you over a shy raised shoulder as she makes the more delicate points. While Bessie is with us, we don't actually have to have records. There was a slip-up in the OPD turmoil once. A rather inarticulate woman, of little will power, was already installed in a bed upstairs before it was discovered that she had only come to sell eggs.

Once I got used to outport speech, I tried to analyze it:

This isn't a dialect or an accent that is spoken here. It's a strong, hearty, vivid language. It doesn't dissipate itself with laziness, illiteracy and intentional quaintness as our mother tongue does in some parts of this continent.

Its starkness is eased by an Irish-like lilt. In its pure form it is hard to come by—like the mating of camels. You will find it, though, in an older fisherman on any of the more isolated islands. Or you can surprise it on the party telephone while waiting for the line to be free.

When it is used in the presence of strangers it is robbed of a little of its colour. Much of the flavour comes from the use of ancient words which appear in Shakespeare, or as the third or fourth definition in Webster. Sometimes they can't be found in any reference book; but that is the fault of the lexicographer, for they issue with the dignity and authority of centuries of accurate meaning.

I have worked with many different groups of people who imparted a high seasoning to the English language: Scotch, Cockney, French Canadian, Italian, Yiddish, Southern, Slavic and Brooklyn. They all have their own charm and music. I like to hear them; but I take care not to let them creep into my speaking.

With outport English it was different:

The Newfoundland speech I earnestly tried to learn and use. Something less than success was the result. The most elusive element was that rhythm and cadence which are the peculiar soul of any language.

Giving up on the rhythm, the next best thing was to adopt the phrases and figures of speech. The ultimate in polite agreement and/or disagreement in response to a statement is "I dare say, I don't know I am sure." This is said in one quick breath with scarcely any pauses between words. There is no rejoinder to that.

Any male from 93 to a new-born (if he has been in the world long enough for a diagnostic glance), is

addressed as 'my son.' The almost equally universal
address 'my dear' does away with sex difference. I was
always pleased to be so spoken to myself, whether by
our laundry women or by a bearded old sea captain.

The world "boy" is used very often in direct conversation. It is softened and shortened to "b'y" and
used with accentuation. One six-year-old patient in a
body cast used to call me "Doctor B'y." Certain phrases have special meanings:

bibber: shiver

bogey-warped: cramped from sitting in one position
near a bogey or small wood stove

burning weather: cold enough to cause frost-bite

clever: handsome, amiable, blustery, strong and
friendly; well-nourished

driving works: raising the devil; cutting up

gall: chafe

glutch: swallow (as in eating, not the bird)

leery: empty in the stomach

lew warm: lukewarm. Archaic Scots or English

neither: used for "any" or "none." "I've neither
copper in the house" means "I'm flat broke."
Frequently shortened to "n'ar," just as "'ar" is used
for "either."

on times, scattered time: occasionally

pitch: This is a nice word. I like this one very
much. It means to settle, find, rest, go down. When
a gale dies, it pitches. When a hovering seagull

settles on a grump or bollard, it pitches. When you fall off your roof, you "pitch" wherever you make contact.

quamish: *on the verge of nausea*

rames: *skeleton or wreck of a vessel, or for that matter a person*

skiver: *skewer or wooden knitting needle*

smurt: *sting*

spawl: *a splinter, especially used of pieces of wood knocked off a mast or keel in a storm*

strained in the head: *demented*

stunned: *slow-minded or dull of wit*

to leg oneself: *to get up after a fall or collapse*

to take your dodge: *to take your time, proceed*

torn up in my mind: *to be confused or undecided, leisurely*

to urge: *to try to vomit*

wonderful: *This word demands special treatment. It is used very often. It means a strong "very." It has no connotation of good. "Wonderful pain," "wonderful sick," wonderful bad." As a matter of fact, it tends to mean bad. If you simply say something is wonderful, chances are it is horrible. It's a combination of Shakespearean accuracy and irony. This word can creep up on you and, before you know it, will appear three times in any paragraph you utter.*

There was a striking lack of vulgarity and profanity. I concluded that it went along with the British inherited habit of understatement:

> When the coastal steamer Clyde was prevented for three days from coming fifteen miles from Herring Neck to Twillingate, the Twillingate Sun reported her as being delayed by "unfavourable breezes." As you hold on to a stanchion to keep yourself from being blown overboard, the polite comment to the captain is "Blows a nice breeze, eh?" The word "dirty" is reserved for weather that isn't even fit for a doctor to be out in.
>
> There is a term that is used to express the ultimate in repulsiveness and evil. I didn't hear it very often because few people or things short of Hitler and an occasional politician are heinous enough to merit this categoric denunciation. The phrase is "It's not good enough." It sounds mild at first, but after knowing people a while and understanding the circumstances that bring out this curse, you can actually feel its impact. In agreement with it you shake your head slowly and expel your breath, expressing more sorrow than anger.

Only one local phrase used to really give me a start. I believe it is also in general British usage. Since I was continually being routed out for night calls, I was frequently hearing the phrase. When a Newfoundlander goes to another person's house in the night with the purpose of making enough noise at the door to arouse him, that process is referred to as "Knocking up." I only mention this to point out that the fault here is clearly American.

The use of the word "tickle" is an interesting one. It is used to designate any comparatively narrow stretch of water connecting two larger bodies of water. If it were larger it would be a strait; Webster does not give a hydrographic definition of the word, but it appears on all the government charts. It might be considered part of a proper name, as Whistle Tickle or Burnt Island Tickle; it is however a definite aquatic entity. The word is used I would suppose because navigation in the tickles is unusually delicate and critical, or, to use Webster's third definition of "ticklish," requiring careful handling.

I myself at age 87 am fortunate to have shared this warm, beautiful scene, whose greatest modern convenience was the radio battery's windcharger, usually mounted on the roof of the house. (I can still hear the windcharger thundering in a stiff breeze, threatening to take the roof with it.) The radio allowed a few to hear from the Outside World, even to hear the BBC, which was doing its innocent bit (despite the static), to modernize the idiom—not always for the better.

As the first-born scion of the British lion, the Newfoundlander has always been comfortable with who he is and what he is—was never drawn into the current quicksand quandary of "self esteem." He or she feels safe to amuse and be amused by recounting and recording the colourful, creative, sometimes quaint, often illuminating, never dull juggling and manipulation of their mother tongue.

Today, however, outport speech is threatened by the unlettered vulgarities of mass communication. Historically and anthropologically, it is important to preserve as much of that speech as we can. Saunders's little book of OPDisms, besides being funny in itself, uncovers yet another facet of the jewel that is Newfoundland English.

Robert Ecke, M. D.
Eliot, Maine
February, 1997

The OPDisms

> *Illness is the night-side of life . . . . Everyone who is born*
> *holds dual citizenship, in the kingdom of the well and in the*
> *kingdom of the sick. Although we all prefer to use*
> *only the good passport, sooner or later each of us is*
> *obliged, at least for a spell, to identify ourselves as*
> *citizens of that other place.*
>
> — Susan Sontag
> *Illness As Metaphor*

One day a female patient, unable to describe precisely how she felt, said: "Well, Doctor, it's like this; when you're sick, you're not well." This apparently inane remark expresses in a few words the unease which every invalid feels. Dr Eric Cassell of Cornell University, in his 1976 book *The Healer's Art*, described it this way:

> The word 'sick' implies not only illness—a feeling
> of unfitness—but a state in which danger to life exists

and urgent action is demanded. One cannot be sick without being ill, but sickness apparently has another dimension. . . . In health we know we are alive by our connectedness to the world. . . . In illness, however slight, some of these contacts are lost. . . . The patient is alternately frightened by the perception of his with-drawal and disinterested in the loss as his horizon shrinks. As he leaves the world of reality, he begins to build a world of his own, an inner world or a world shared exclusively with other sick. Sometimes the new world may be so appealing that return from its simpler delights may be difficult. . . .

Like any rural physician, Dr Olds had learned a lot since med school. He had learned, for instance, the importance of knowing what poultice a patient swore by. Before the advent of modern antibiotics after World War II, the poultice was a stan-dard home remedy. Using them, skilled women cured infected wounds, fevers, inflammations and chest disorders. A poultice might be made from mustard plaster, moldy bread, fried onions, molasses, oatmeal, fir bark, linseed meal—or some mail-order concoction like *Antiflogestine.* Some poultices worked, others didn't. When they didn't, it was usually because the condition was too serious—a TB-induced fever, or typhoid, or diphthe-ria—or because the user was inexperienced or gave up too soon. From the condition of poultice and patient, Dr Olds often gleaned vital clues to the nature and progress of a disease.

Olds had also learned never to ask, "What seems to be the trouble?" or "What is wrong with you?" To all such queries the answer was nearly always, "Doctor, that's for you to tell *me.*" Instead, he used the local idiom: "What do you find?" In other words, what symptoms to you feel? With this golden key he unlocked the patient's story—and now and then a gem of wit.

Sometimes the wit was intentional, as when he asked a

Twillingate South Island man about his recent prostate operation:

"Can you pass urine all right now?"

"Yes, doctor."

"A good stream?"

"Doctor, I could piss over to the North Side!" (The two islands are separated by a tickle many metres across.)

Usually the humour was unintentional, as when the woman from Whale's Gulch exclaimed, "Doctor, me nerves is teetotally gone!"

Startling turns of phrase cropped up in the most serious discussions:

"How are your bowels?"

"My bowels are as regular as my breakfast."

Or: "I have an automatic voice; it cuts in and it cuts out."

"We touch heaven when we lay our hand on a human body."

— Norvalis

Often it was the attempt to use an unfamiliar word or expression that tripped them up. Asked whether she had ever had an operation, a woman replied, "Yes, I had a repair of my virginia." A man, incensed at his long wait in Outpatients, called the delay "impatientable." A man with a mangled finger said, "Oh, I cut it with the drill. It was going very fast—at least 40 RPM per minute."

Patient: "Doctor, I've had two or three heart attacks."

Olds: "Really?"

Patient: "Yes, but no *lethal* ones."

A mother explained that she wanted her husband to go see a doctor, "if only to get his 'composition.'" Another complained of a bad head since taking two "noxine" [inoculation] needles for diphtheria. The woman who said she had been "ministrating" for seven days of course meant menstruating. The mother who asked for some "conversation" medicine for her little boy meant constipation medicine. Meningitis in a letter became "manajoyides." The man who said Dr Olds had diagnosed a bad case of "pepsical" ulcers meant to say peptic.

Somewhere, one patient had picked up the expression "heart pyleogram." Another spoke of "scarlateen fever" [scarlatina or scarlet fever]. There were many other confusions:

"I had the catarrah [catarrh] and compulsions [convulsions]."

"The barnacle [varicose] veins in my legs bothers me a lot."

"I wants some salve for linge taylo, or is it infatiger?" [impetigo]

"Something rises up in my stomach and I can't regest [digest] any food."

"I wants to know if Father has a vagina [angina] heart."

"I got out of my refinement [confinement] case alright but have been sick ever since."

Olds and his team had to be able to translate.

Olds: "What was your operation for?"
Patient: "I had an explosion [exploratory] operation on my kidney."

"I borned two bleaches at home, Doctor" [two breach-births, i.e., babies born feet first].

"She was under the compression [impression] that she had something growing in her."

Or: "Yes, I have been wearing an uplift [support for early inguinal hernia] for a long time."

Or: "I had a heart attack and I was in a noxygen tank for seventy-two hours."

"My daughter got her neck strained up from using a left-handed cash register."

"She put a stick [tongue depressor] down her throat and broke the flammation on her stomach."

A young woman, successfully operated on for tonsils and adenoids and wanting to go home, asked: "When will I be delivered?"

"My God," said Olds, "I didn't know you were in for that!" Turning to the R. N., he said, "Did you know that?" The nurse replied, "No, John; she means discharged."

With so much verbal confusion in the air, sometimes the nurses got talking the same way. A worried daughter who had just visited her sick mother on the women's ward took out her fears on the nurse. The nurse then vented on Dr Olds: "That woman's daughter keeps complaining! Now she says her mother is dirty. Well, the woman gets bathed every morning, so as far as I'm concerned the dirt must have been there before she came in. . . ."

At times the humour sprang from misinformation about a disease, a test or a treatment. "Doctor," said an inpatient, "I am afraid to take my barium enema. Could I drink it instead?" A patient in considerable pain exclaimed: "I got arthritis, Doctor; have it in my head and in every nerve of my body!" After a urine test another said, "Is there any sign of arthritis in my water, doctor?"

Take a small stick and cut on it as many notches as you have
warts, then put it in the ground, and as it rots
the warts will disappear.

— Old Dorset County charm

Often it was awkward phrasing that enclosed a grain of truth. An anemic woman wanted her blood tested "because it must be low."

"Why must it be low?"

"Because, when I sticks a needle in myself I don't bleed nearly as much as I used to." Another said, "Doctor, I wants to know if my blood has evaporated again." Yet another said, "When I gets anemic I have a craving for dry cereal. I could eat it all day long."

Usually the expression came out of the kind of contorted logic so common in Newfoundland humour: "I have an aching in my chest just before I wakes up in the mornings."

Olds: "Are your periods regular?"
Patient: "They haven't been, but the last time it was."

Sometimes it was plain neurosis: "I goes to bed early to get away from meself." Mostly it was just a lively sense of metaphor: "How are you today, George?"

"Not bad, Doctor; but I believe my memory has capsized."

Patient: "I faints when I gets a fright."
Olds: "Oh? What frightens you?"
Patient: "I got a fright when a horse flashed 'is hinders at me." It *is* a scary sight.

Some patients got to like the hospital's friendly atmosphere. There was one old woman with various ailments, among them a condition that she called "arthritis in the breast." In November, as the time for the coastal vessel's last trip before freeze-up approached, she showed signs of staying for the winter. Nurse Margo Drover asked Dr Olds if he knew any reason why she shouldn't go home.

"None," he said, "if you can get her to go." So Margo went to talk to her.

"Oh, I can't go yet, maid," said the woman. "I haven't had me X-ray." In those days many patients thought of X-rays not as a diagnostic tool but as somehow part of the cure. So Margo took her to the X-ray department, flicked a few lights, told her it was done, and she went home content.

"Every observant practitioner knows that he treats patients rather than diseases."
— Dr Alfred Stille

The remaining OPDisms relate to many parts of the human body and to the psyche as well. Because for women it was an era of hard physical labour and the bearing of many children, female complaints predominate.

Come sit now with Olds in Outpatients, as he takes the world in for repairs. Here comes the first patient of the day. . .

"And what do you find. . .?"

Eye, Ear, Nose & Throat

D r Olds examined eyes, prescribed glasses and removed cataracts. Eye complaints ranged from silly symptoms like, "My eyes squinch up when I gets a haircut," to serious ailments like glaucoma and cataracts. Always there were some who needed glasses, or who thought they did.

At one end of the Outpatient Department Dr Olds had set up an eye-testing machine, a very good model. To use it properly it was necessary that the patient sit in this high-backed chair, a certain distance from the screen, with the head snug against the head-rest.

For some reason a lot of women dressed up for eye examinations. Some considered curlers an asset. But the curlers prevented their heads from fitting snugly. When this happened, Dr

Olds would stalk out, call the Outpatients Officer and say, "Ernie, tell her to get those godammed curlers out!'"

One cantankerous old man, asked why he wouldn't go to Gander as recommended, replied contemptuously: "I been there two or three times—they wanted to take my eyes out of me head, scrope 'em, and put 'em back in again." ("Excision of cataracts," wrote Olds.)

Another eye patient complained about the cost: "I had my eyes tested by an optimistic and paid $80.00 for the glasses, and they went squish and I couldn't wear them."

One woman returned her glasses with this explanation, "When I went anywhere, it was like the door was coming towards me." Another had a mysterious pain when she wore her glasses: "I finds it in the balls o' me eyes," she explained. "Seems it comes out of me 'ead." And a young man suffered from a curious side effect: "When he reads too much, his jaws snap together and he has to quit." A woman who suffered from some sort of fit explained, "When the attack is passing over me, I haven't got the visibility."

A mother brought in a young man with "a roarin' in 'is 'ead." It was so bad, she said, that when she put her ear up to his, she could hear it too. Another patient heard a softer sound in his skull. Asked to describe it, he allowed it sounded like fish frying.

Said a pleased but puzzled husband, "The wife dropped a brick on her toe and couldn't open her mouth."

To swallow, as Dr Ecke had discovered, was to *glutch*.

Patient: "Doctor, there's something wrong with me throat."
Doctor: "Oh? What do you feel?"
Patient: "I can't glutch."

As so often happens in English, a verb can also be a noun: "Can't find me glutch, Doctor; oh my."

An old woman "swallowed the corner of a biscuit and it is still there!"

Go to a young tree; cut a slit in the tree; cut off a bit of your hair and put it under the rind [bark]; put your hand to the tree and say to it: "This I bequeath...in the name of the Father, and of the Son, and of the Holy Ghost. Amen."

— Old Dorset toothache charm

A mother brought her little girl, saying, "She has a red throat and kernels in her neck" [strep throat with swollen lymph nodes].

Another deplored his bad breath: "It wakes me up at night and I have a mouth like an outdoor toilet in the morning."

"My daughter had trouble with her throat," said a housewife. "She couldn't swallow and they put a tube down which went all the way to her rectory."

Respiratory

The sharp compassion of the healer's art
Resolving the enigma of the fever chart.

—T.S. Eliot
Four Quartets

The expression "shortness of breath" covered a spectrum of ailments. "I get a lump in my breath," declared a middle-aged fisherman. "You are short-breathed?" said Dr Olds. "I was always short-breathed," said he. "My brother had to nudge me at night; I always slept with short breath."

"I gets giddy," said another, "short of breath, with an acheness in my chest." A young man explained, "I finds my breath only—my throat I finds gone, but perfectly well in health."

One elderly man described his emphysema thus: "I got no breath, see; a germ got more breath than I have." Other variations on this theme are:

"I am a wonderful person to draw my breath heavy."

"I can't hardly get enough breath to draw."

Olds: "Do you ever get short of breath?"
Patient: "Only when I'm asleep, Doctor."

A woman who had been struck by lightning years ago complained of laboured night breathing [sleep apnea]. Her cure was to "pull my tongue and rub my hands together until I feel better."

Some judged the state of their lungs by how well they could climb a hill. "I gets so short-breathed I can't walk up a hill the length of meself," said one. Said another, "Doctor, I can't face a hill; I have to back up or I get short-breathed."

Heart

In Dr Olds's day, heart cases were referred to St John's or to a mainland specialist, a decision involving a costly journey not yet covered by medical insurance. His decision would be based on symptoms such as these:

"The pain in my left side is so bad, it pulls me heart down and makes it flutter."

"My heart pumps a lot of gas and hurts my stomach."

Patient: "I have a pain in my chest."
Olds: "Very bad?"
Patient: "No; oh no, I'm not *dangerous*, Doctor."
Doctor: "Anybody in your family with heart troubles?"
Patient: "Yes, Mother had it; but not during the last seven years."
Doctor: "She was cured?"
Patient: "No—she died."

One patient was so convinced he had heart trouble that he came several times a year to Dr Olds for an examination. But Olds couldn't find anything wrong with him. Finally the man said, "Well, it must be something. The heart is bating, bating fast, bating all the time."

"Goddamit," said Olds, "'tis better for it to beat fast than not beat at all!"

Patient: "I would like to have a heart test."
Doctor: "What kind do you want?"
Patient: "I wants a autograph test."

Afterward the patient said, "Well, doctor, how many bad hearts do I got?"

Gastro-Intestinal

Many OPDisms refer to stomach ailments. "I am foolish enough," said a nervous patient, "to think I have arthritis in my stomach." A man said: "Yes, I did have arthritis—years ago, before I was born."

Doctor: "What is wrong with the baby?"
Mother: "He got a cold in his teeth and the hot water went to his stomach." ["Baby has no teeth," noted Olds.]

"My boy," said another, "has had pains in the stomach all summer. The doctor was down Sunday before last and took a load of his manure to examine."

Examining a male patient with odd symptoms, Dr Olds asked "Does any kind of food bother you?"

"I don't think so," he replied, "I eat the same food off and on."

To a female patient he said, "Does fatty food bother you?" She replied, "Yes, I ate a banana and it nearly killed me!"

Despite their ignorance of medical terminology, patients often came up with very apt descriptions. "I've got titters in my bumbo, Doc!" said a male patient. [*Pruritis ani*, noted Olds.] This woman's account of a gall bladder attack was not only colourful but fairly accurate: "When I eats grease," said she, "it goes to my head and it gets numb; I gets tightness in my stomach when I walks, and it goes to my rectum and itches."

A man with a bleeding ulcer noted that his stools were "black as a telephone." (Most telephones were black then.)

However, some of the explanations which patients devised were odd, to say the least. Asked whether she ever vomited, a young woman explained, "No, doctor; it comes up by itself as the liver gets hold of it and throws it back." A bartender diagnosed his bad stomach: "I think it's due to a change in the beer."

Doctor: "How are you today?"
Patient: "Alright, except I have the 'stinky belks.'"
[belches]

"When I vomits in the stove," observed another, "it tisses almost like gas!" [Dr Story defines "tiss" as "to hiss, to fizz."]

A child said, "I had a bad pain in my stomach last night as big as my fist." Another accurately described the onset of nausea as, "I have a sickly feeling in the mouth."

One man brought in his son because the child had swallowed "a machine." Questioned as to its nature, he described it as "part of a pleasure thing, a contrivance for making a noise, a part of a horn the size of a dime."

Sometimes the humour came from the other direction. A child was brought in after supposedly swallowing a quarter. After taking an X-ray, the intern examined it and said to her mother, "Ma'am, I'm afraid there's no change on the X-ray."

Stomach and bowel ailments are a recurrent theme in the notebooks, especially constipation. "I goes a long time without using my bowels," explained an old man. Said a pulp cutter, "My bowels only works every five or six days. I s'pose hard work doos that."

"Well," growled a retired sea captain, "me bowels is stuck, Sir. T'other day, I 'ad to force 'em somethin' wonderful." A housewife allowed she was "wonderful constipated," adding, "I can't get anything without taking passage." Another woman described her migraine symptoms in this way: "Doctor, that's me constipation headache, not me normal headache."

On the subject of regularity, Dr Olds preferred to be oblique; but that was not always possible. A very constipated woman had arrived by boat one evening and been treated. Next morning on rounds, he asked her if she had "passed anything." "Yes, Doctor," she said with no trace of a smile, "I passed a skiff with a punt in tow." Olds reworded his question: "Did you shit, if you know what I mean?" Another patient said she was so constipated she couldn't change her breath, "had to breathe two or three times before it would change."

Then there was diarrhea. "Are your bowels the same every day?" asked Olds. "No, they are not bad every day," replied the patient.

"I took a little salts," said another, "got a wonderful tearing away feeling—and then had a removement of my bowels."

The following exchange took place after a woman complained of "wind and pain in my 'interstitials' [intestines]:"

Dr Olds: "Do your bowels work all right?"
Patient: "I had diarrhea when I first went home, but they are more reconciled now."

Loss of appetite accounted for many entries.

Olds: "Is her appetite good?"
Patient's husband: "No, she only eats a little and not much o' that."

A husband observed that once in a while his wife would come up with a good appetite, "but not a ravishing one." Said a woman with dietary quirk: "I can't eat butter since poor Father died fourteen years ago; it turned me against it!"

Dr Olds: "Is your appetite good?"
Patient: "Sir, my appetite is too strong for me!"

Then as now, the vermiform appendix was a source of trouble. Because it could flare up without much warning and most patients lived in isolated communities, Twillingate doctors routinely removed it during abdominal surgery whether it was inflamed or no.

There were exceptions. "Seven years ago," said a father who had just brought in his son with acute appendicitis, "the doctor told him he had the appendix but it wasn't ripe enough to take out."

In that era of hard physical work and frequent child-bearing, many men and women suffered from hemorroids, popularly known as "piles." A man allowed that his piles felt much better since the nurses had been putting ointment on his "directum." Another wrote in to say, "I would like to get some pile plugs [suppositories]."

Doctor: "How is your husband now?"
Woman: "Oh, he is like Balaam in the Bible—he has trouble with his ass."

A nervous female patient described her symptoms as "weakness in back and titters in my bum hole."

"All my life," complained an old fisherman, "I never had much water power."

A man allowed he felt much better after being catheterized and having passed "1,000 calories of urine."

Sometimes they misunderstood the diagnosis: "The doctor told me I had water in me bladder."

"When I passes my water," said an older woman, "the burning in my legs gets better—I think it is connected with my backer passage—but I gets all dizzy."

Doctor: "You say you've had water trouble for two months?"
Patient: "Yes, I pass my water far too often—twice a week."

A mother brought her child to "find out if she was a real bed-wetter or was her kidneys weak."

It is a demographic fact that where poverty and ignorance abound, people have more children. A dozen or more to a family was not unusual in the 1930s and 1940s. John Shillito Jr, a

Harvard medical student who spent the summer of 1952 in Twillingate, remarked, "It was not an uncommon frustration to ask a middle-aged multiparous woman in late pregnancy when her last menstrual period had occurred, and to be stopped with the reply: 'Doctor, when I was thirteen!'"

Dr Ecke described one young Fogo woman, "wan, pretty. . . with a faraway voice, hair coming down, stockings coming down, bathrobe and slippers. . . wandering vaguely around among the wreckage produced by eight children. 'I have too many, Doctor,' she says, 'I don't know where they all comes from!'"

When Olds asked one female patient whether she had any children, she replied, "No. Oh, yes; I had one two years ago." After informing another that she had the itch or scabies and that the whole family must be treated, he asked, "How many have you in family?"

"Hmm. . . " she mused, "I think fourteen."

Patient: "Do you think, Doctor, I can have my baby by myself?"

Doctor: "Yes, didn't you say you had no trouble last time?"

Patient: "I had no trouble except I fractured my womb. . . . Well, it said on my discharge paper 'ruptured membrane.'"

The doctor asked a pregnant woman whether she had any pain anywhere. "No, Sir," she replied, "but I hurts down here." [Pointing to lower abdomen]

Said one whose child had been ill: "I'm going to leave the baby in the hospital until he gets really better. My first baby was in so often I had to bring him back sometimes before he was discharged."

For many unmarried young women, the causes of pregnancy seemed elusive—or so they let on. Said one: "I got my
feet wet picking berries in the burnt woods and my periods
stopped." Another, asked when her last period had occurred,
said, "I don't rightly know—but I think it was about bakeapple-
picking time." A third, informed she was pregnant and asked
whether she was expecting that, replied: "I don't know, doctor. I
work in the fish plant and thought I caught a cold." A woman
brought in her young daughter to see Dr Olds, telling him that
she had "passed colours twice" [vaginal bleeding]. As he
entered the examining room, the girl was crying. He soon estab-
lished that she was pregnant and told them so. "Doctor," said
the mother grimly, "she be cryin' now for last year's laughter!"

Another desperate girl asked if he did "absorptions."
Questioned as to where her mother was, she shot back, "I never
'ad nar [neither] mother!" Another declared, "That woman doctor said I's pregnant, but she be soft in the 'ead." But another
said matter-of-factly: "I think I am bred three months." Olds
heard it all.

Married women's complaints took more telling. Unfami-
liarity with medical terms was one reason; but mostly they were
shy about discussing intimate details with a male doctor. Even
talking to a female doctor unnerved some. One young woman

who was excitedly telling a female doctor about her mother-in-law's symptoms suddenly stopped short, hand to mouth: "My goodness, listen to me, talking to you like you was an ordinary woman!"

A typical delicate exchange with a male doctor went like this:

Doctor: "You say you have had some bleeding?"
Patient: "Yes, Doctor. But the blood didn't come from my water passage."
Doctor: "What passage did it come from then?"
Patient: "Er. . . it came from my intercourse passage."

"I've been bleeding from my lower passages," said another woman, "but I don't know whether it's from my backside or the moon."

Olds: "Are you having any medicines?"
Woman: "No, I had a hysterectomy."

Recounting the stages of her recent delivery, a patient said, "I had 'corruption' [rupture of membranes] on Tuesday." A new mother who had seen women boiling baby bottles, asked why she wasn't breast-feeding her baby, replied, "Well, I can't scald my nipples now, can I?" Said one, "I have had a vaginal discharge ever since I had my tonsils out."

And one patient gave this description of severe menstrual cramps: "About that time of the month, I gets so bad I could walk up my own legs!"

Understandably perhaps, some women admitted to a distaste for sex. "My face goes squish when my husband reaches his climax," said one, "and I wants to throw up." She should have had a heart-to-heart with the woman who told Dr Olds, "I'm weak all over. 'Tis my husband's fault; he be too heavy for me, five and six times a night." Another complained, "My husband has too much manpower."

A male patient, trying to explain what ailed his wife, declared, "She finds some wonderful complaints, Doctor. I think she ought to come to the Hospital." Another man came out with this puzzler:

Doctor: "Did you ever have an operation?"
Patient: "Well, I am not sure. . . . My wife had a little operation on her ovary. . . ."

Menopause or "change of life"—one woman called it the *unchange* of life—brought its share of symptoms. "Do you have hot flashes?" asked the doctor of a 47-year-old woman. "No," she said, "I am too cold all the time to have hot flashes." Said another, "My hands have been so cold I didn't know nobody."

Men brought their share of sexual worries too. Said one patient, "I am afraid my bird will get so small I can't make my water out of it. I want a X-ray on it and maybe you can strap it up and help me."

"Doctor," said one, "My testicle is in two parts it seems." ['*Cyst epididymis*,' wrote Olds.]

"My nature is down," said another man. "I'm just as much for a woman but I don't rise up—at least not enough— and 'tis wonderful tormentin'." One man, apparently delighted by the sexual side effects of a medicine, said: "I wants some more of they pills."

Prostate trouble brought many older men to Outpatients. Occasionally they dared to question Dr Olds's work. "I had my prostate gland out last month," said one, "and now I can't hold my water at all; did 'e put my bladder back after the opertion?"

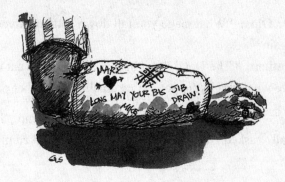

"My arm is very sore when I bends it, Doctor. I have to sleep with it straight out. 'Tis a good job my wife has two legs—I sleeps with it over her top leg."

Bad backs were a much more prolific source of comments. A man said of his wife: "She has a bad back and can't stand over her water [i.e., can't straighten up] after she makes it." One patient discovered a novel remedy: "The pain in my back is so bad I have to nip my nose."

The husband of one patient described odd interfaces between bladder and lungs and vertebrae: "After she passes her water in the morning, she takes a breath and finds it in her back." A man explained, "When I takes pills they goes out in my joints and connects with my water."

A patient declared she was so stiff she "had to help the nurse get me on the bed." Another allowed, "My back is so bad I have to get down on the floor to get up." The mother of a young store clerk asked: "Would wrapping up parcels give my daughter a bad arm? She does a lot; some days she does up $2,000 worth."

Falling and breaking bones elicited some novel explanations.

Dr Olds: "What made you fall down and break your arm again?"

Patient: "The Devil did it because he didn't want me to see what was in the pot." [Presumably a chamber pot]

A 73-year-old lady had fallen and broken her hip. "How did you fall?" asked Olds. Said she, "The Spirit knocked me over."

Sleep Disorders, Etc.

Asked if she slept well, a woman with multiple complaints replied, "Yes; my sleep don't seem to hurt me." Explained another, "It's like my sleep is too strong for my nerves."

One man thought he had discovered a cure for night cramps in his legs: "I put some silver in my bed."

"What kind of silver do you put in?"

"I put in a dime. It doesn't cost much and it works; two or three people told me about it."

Said another, "I get the shakelies at night and also gets dizzified."

"Every now and again there's a pain in under my left breast and he lefts then and goes over on my right side."

From the OPD, many patients were admitted for further testing or for surgery. One elderly woman protested, "Oh no, doctor, I can't stay—I didn't bring my knitting."

If a patient had just come through major surgery, Olds would be anxious to hear in their own words how they felt. He might enter with his clipboard and drawl, "Well, skipper, how are you this morning?" If the doctor was lucky he might hear some variation of this response: "Doctor, I never felt no finer!"

However, what with the pain and the post-ether nausea, most felt rotten and said so. Some were more creative. One eighty-year-old man paused significantly, then said, "Doctor, I believe I could kill a man right now if he made me mad enough."

Olds liked the Zen-like depth of this woman's reply: "Well, my dear, I'd have to get better to be dead."

Mind Games

In Olds's day the Hospital had no psychiatrist. People aired their mental woes anyway. "The doctor told my father I had a cross current in my brain when I was fourteen years old, and my mind has been bad ever since."

Some, like Moses, were slow of speech: "I have to talk twice before I can get the right word out."

Olds: "And what's wrong with you?"
Patient: "I came to get cured of my short-mindedness."

Said another, "My fucking memory is gone; I just lost it then."

One old man who lived alone was tormented by rascally boys but found a remedy: "I chopped me apple trees down."

"Chopped them down, John?"

"Yes, they boys used to come and steal me apples in the night, so I chopped 'em down."

Marital tensions surfaced. A woman complained of her husband's crankiness: "He gets so mad you have to take your words out of your mouth and look at them before you dare to speak."

An old diabetic woman was crying. "What's the matter?" asked the doctor. "I have been married fifty years," she sobbed, "and if I had my time back I wouldn't have had him."

Though brain surgery was not attempted at Twillingate, Dr Olds performed such emergency operations as removing bone fragments from fractured skulls, and relieving pressure caused by concussions or water on the brain. Still, plenty of other head ailments turned up at Outpatients.

A menopausal woman said, "I finds me 'ead some wonderful my dear." The doctor asked how long she had suffered headaches. "I don't find it now," she replied. "Mostly I finds it when it takes me."

Another woman described a friend who had recently recovered from mental illness: "She had to go to St. John's seventeen years ago, didn't know she was there, and when she came round she thought she was in the *Titanic*."

A man confessed to attempting suicide. "I was going to jump over the wharf and make away with myself, when I looked around and seed there wasn't any water—'twas frozen over."

Epilepsy seems to have been more common than it is today, and certainly it was far less treatable. Dr Olds copied down one sufferer's description of a *grand mal* seizure: "I had an 'ipical' fit and my eyeballs turned upside down and bubbles came out of my mouth." He also recorded this patient's explanation of her epilepsy: "I used to have fits, especially when my blood turned from winter condition to summer."

A woman explained, "When I presses heavy on my heels I gets dizzy." Another, suffering from the similar spells, was asked whether she knew beforehand when they were coming. "Yes, Sir," she said, "my water gets right yellow about three days before."

"There is hardly a man living, be his disease what it may, who will bear to believe himself beyond the possibility of restoration to health."

—Dr. Peter M. Latham
Lectures on Clinical Medicine

Senility

A mong the most poignant entries are those from the aged and dying. From spring through fall, when small boats could travel freely and the weather was warmer, many elderly patients came to the Hospital. Those who made it to old age in the days of high infant mortality were often remarkably fit; but like most old people they had many aches and pains. Most came to see Dr Olds, whom they knew in person or by reputation. But of course he could not see them all.

To deal with this big summer influx, he relied on summer students from American medical schools like Johns Hopkins or Harvard, and, in later years, from Memorial University. One of these was James A. Pittman Jr, later to become Dean of the University of Alabama School of Medicine. Dr Pittman's journal for July 5, 1951 describes what it was like: "OPD all day—

madhouse. All the patients over 80 with innumerable aches & pains, each of which each tried not only to enumerate but to describe in poetic detail. Did, however, admit child with TB, [a man] with testicular tumour; [also] referred pt. to Montreal Neurological Institute, & sent pt. to sanatorium."

Said an elderly man, "I have pains in my face and they go down into my false teeth just like a toothache."

An eighty-nine-year old lady, stripped to the waist in the examining room and shivering violently, felt she had the 'flu.

Doctor: "Are you aching?"
Patient: (Shivering): "Yes."
Doctor: "All over?"
Patient: (Still shivering): "No, it's not all over yet; that's why I came up."

Another old lady cheerfully announced she was ready to meet her Maker. "It's time I died," she declared. "The angel come for me yesterday, Sir; but I had a bad stomach and couldn't go." On soiling her bed, she explained to the aide: "My dear, they got lovely toilets in Heaven. And in Heaven I would have made it to the toilet, for St. Peter would have held the door for me. I wants to go to Heaven, dear, but they won't cut off me cable [catheter]. I can't go to Heaven with that cable now, can I?"

One day on rounds Dr Olds complimented a male patient on his rapid recovery: "You've done well, Dorman. You were sick all right."

"Yes, Doctor; I did very well for a dead man."

Miscellany

*"For all the physick we can use, art, excellent industry, is to
no purpose without calling on God: it is vain to seek for help,
run, hide, except God bless us. Hippocrates, an heathen,
required this in a good practitioner,
and so did Galen."*

—Richard Burton
Anatomy of Melancholy

The notebooks contain many sayings that fit no particular
category. For example, a man suffering from extreme
ulceration of the hard palate made such a rapid recovery that
Olds complimented him: "Gus, you must live right!" To which
Gus humbly replied, "Well, doctor, I do—except when I gets
tangled up."

"I'm weak, doctor," said one. "I've had four 'flus this winter." Boasted another, "I had a dose of the 'flu but I killed it
with aspirin tablets."

A mother described her anemic son as being "so tired he

has to have a spell to pick up the telephone receiver." One patient complained of weakness in the knees: "They got so bad last night that I had to get up and open the window." Another said, "My strength is very weak and I have germs going through my ears."

One man, told he did not have diabetes, gave the traditional Newfoundland blessing: "Sir, long may your big jib draw!"

During the Great Depression, parents with big families were often unable to feed their children properly. At one house Dr Ecke diagnosed rickets, a softening of the bones due to lack of Vitamin D or calcium or both. "That's funny," said the mother. "I gives 'em cod liver oil, six spoons a day."

"For how long?" he asked.

"Since Thursday," said she.

A patient late for his appointment gave this excuse: "I went over to Piercey's [Hotel] for to stay and I got myself over-slept." A woman, asked if she had any pain, replied testily, "No, I made two pairs of pants last week, so I couldn't have [had] much pain." Another female patient, perhaps preoccupied with a bake sale, said, "I have a nervous lump on me sweet-breads." One irritated patient asked, "Is Dr Dennison here? I never seen him so scarce."

Like most experienced physicians, Olds knew how to sift the genuine from the imaginary. There was one Twillingate woman who used to come to the Hospital thirty or forty times a year, always with some minor complaint or other. One time she came in to Outpatients with her arm "all swole up."

"And what do you think caused that?" asked Dr Olds.

"A fly bit me, Doctor," she said, pleased at having a real ailment to parade for once.

"Well, where's the fly?"

"What do you mean, Doctor?"

"How the hell can I treat you if you didn't bring the fly?"

And there were many who just wanted a sympathetic listener. "I feel that weak, my tongue is clove to the roof of my mouth and my leg is all drawed up and whatnot and I don't know what I will do in the world at all whatever." A bed-ridden woman moaned, "I can't walk. I smurt and burn and ache all over; my hands, my feet, my side, my back, my stomach. But I baint [be not] quite numb."

The common cold was good for many visits. Few brought so unusual an excuse as this man: "See, I was working on the road for Town Council, and there was hardly enough work to keep warm."

Letters

Sometimes Olds saved letters: "Please excuse my bad writing," wrote a patient in a cast, "as I can only write with one hand."

A man explained his symptoms:

> *I can't tell 'e exactly how I feels, Doctor; I finds a sort of a dead pain, you know, a 'hakein' an' a smurtin' an' a burnin.' It starts here and runs around 'ere and stops 'ere by the little spot where me gun exploded six years ago. I only finds it when I works and if you don't mind would 'e give me a 'tificate so I can git a bit of food for me 'n the old woman?*

A slip of paper inserted in the 1943 notebook makes this irresistible plea: "Doctor, could you loan me [Olds deleted the amount] dollars? I'd rather owe you the money then anybody else."

One man wrote: "Could you forward me the following: Salve or ointment or some treatment for scurvy, piles, ingrowing toe nails. Please enclose bill. . . ." A woman with a weight problem wrote: "Please send enough of those slimy pills; I have lost six pounds."

Another wrote grandly of her many illnesses:

To Doctor Olds, Memorial Hospital.

> *Dear Sir - It give me great Pleasure to write you these few Lines to let you know how I am feeling now in health. Well Doc I am not the Best now at Present as I*

*always have a Bad Head an it Causes a pain Right
Down to the End of my Swallow. My throat and Breast
Bothers me so much and by times I do have hot flashes
and other times I do be Cold, not much swelling now
Just a little some times. I am sending down to you Sir to
send me up some medicine one Bottle of liquid and 50
cts worth of heart tablets.*

> *1 Bottle of liquid
> 50 cts worth of heart tablets.*

I thank you. I am yours sincerely,

A merchant put on paper this delicate family matter:

Dear Sir,

   *It may seem rather vulgar to approach anyone in
this way, but my son would prefer doing this to permit-
ting or telling his ailment. It seems he has some sort of
contagious disease in the penis, probably a dose, clapp
if you like.*
   I regret to approach you in this manner.

> *Yours truly. . .*

One man felt like a leper in his own community:

Dear Dr Olds,

   *I am writing you concerning myself the discharge is
all cleared up and I never used the tablets I am writing
you to ask you if you will please send back and tell me
that I am a clean person the people of Shoe Cove Brook
said that I had a bad disease and that is why the Dr. in
Twillingate would not take me in hospital I always
thought that was the place to go for anything and would
you be kind enough to write back and say I had no disease that I have clean body send as soon as possible*

because I am hurted a lot to see what the people is reporting and not true please oblige and send me a report.

> *Yours truely. . .*

Of course, even by mail there were malingerers. This one wanted to change doctors:

> *I was down to the Hospital on the 16 of April for Examination and I understand that you were resting, so Dr. Woods Examined me and told me I had Severe Male Climatimic; Gastericic.*
>
> *Well, he gave me tablets for the change in me and a medicine for my Stomach but I find my back bad all the Time, from the Time I took the flue Feb. 16 until now and its still getting worse I told Dr Woods I felt my back awful bad and I was taking Gin Pills and he told me my kidneys weren't bad and there wasn't any need of taking anything; but Dr Olds if my kidneys is not bad it must be the spine. Some days I am not able to get around the House. As for my Stomach, that is not as bad as it was but my head and back is no better. . . . Now Dr Olds I want you if you are able and willing to Examine me if I come down but in the meantime I can't get down unless you send up for me to come down for Examination, and Ill send it to the Relieving Officer in Lewisporte and Ill get a pass to come down on.*
>
> *Now Dr Olds perhaps it would be best if Dr Woods dosnt know I wrote you about my condition seeing he's treating me. . . .*

Another man suffered from a spectrum of complaints:

> *I haven't done any work since I left Twillingate Hospital. I am not feeling any better, all I can do is to*

*walk around the door, and the more I walk the worse I
get, and I also swell in the hands. After I am resting all
night the next morning I am feeling a little better. But
after I get up for about half an hour and start moving
around, I get boiling hot in the head and come out red
in the face. My head is paining all the time and I
become weak. My stomach is still bad and my food still
hurts me. About hour or hour and a half after I get up,
my food goes sour. I finds a wonderful lot of pain in my
stomach and the most I finds in on my left sidearound
the heart. Most all the food I eat hurts me and the only
food which don't hurt me is whole wheat bread [Dole
ration] when its toasted. When I try to do anything the
heart beats so fast I get sick and weak. The bottle of
medicine you sent me didn't seem to do me any good.
Could you write and tell me what causes my head to be
always hot and the food to go sour in my stomach, and
also weak feelings. I am losing weight because I can't
eat anything. If you like to ask me a few questions about
my troubles I would only be glade to answer them. If
you send any Drugs please send it C.O.D.*

One man gave a long list of symptoms, complained that
another doctor was no good, and concluded: "You told me to
come down as soon as possible, but I won't. I'll go to Botwood
Hospital. I went to you before, and all you done was swore and
told me I was 'nervess.'"

Hospital Food

No collection of hospital sayings would be complete without comments on the food. Probably Notre Dame Bay Memorial was no better in this regard than most hospitals, at least not after it stopped growing its own. For a decade or two after it opened its doors in 1924, it was nearly self-sufficient. It kept certified milch cows, and a few pigs and hens to recycle kitchen scraps. There was no shortage of fresh milk, cream, butter and eggs, nor of ham, bacon, poultry and an occasional beef. It grew rhubarb, potatoes, cabbage, beets, turnips and carrots, and canned a lot of greens. Moreover, under Olds's Blanket Contract—a pioneering form of medical insurance he started in 1934—people could pay their hospital bills "in kind." So there was a steady flow of fish, vegetables and berries to be stored in its root cellars and freezers.

In those years the complaints were more apt to be about the strangeness of the food than about its quality. Before the advent of sulfa drugs (1935), penicillin (1940) and the later antibiotics (1946), not to mention vitamin tablets, food was a major weapon in curing illness, especially tuberculosis. Doctors and nurses made every effort to get essential vitamins into patients' diets, particularly Vitamins A (for eye problems and night blindness), B (for beriberi, etc.), C (for scurvy, etc.) and D (for rickets).

For A and D, daily doses of cod liver oil (which patients dubbed "God Oil") were prescribed—and generally abhorred. The B complex was supplied by brewer's yeast and brown flour. Patients said the yeast "tasted bad" (it does), and that the whole wheat bread "did not look good, did not taste good and was not white."

According to Olds, eating brown bread also carried a social sigma: "If you ate it you had to be on the Dole [welfare]. It represented hard times." This stigma dated back to 1933, when the government in St John's, warned by Dr Olds and his predecessor Dr Charles Parsons, moved to stop a beriberi outbreak in the outports. They replaced the vitamin-less white flour with whole wheat flour in Dole rations. The move stopped the epidemic in its tracks; but the stigma remained.

"The old people were so set in their ways," mused Olds in the 1970s. "They wouldn't eat the fresh cod, and they wouldn't look at a mackerel to save their life. Fresh herring was the same. At the Hospital we couldn't afford orange juice, so we bought tomato juice, the next best thing. The barrels of it we had to throw away! They just wouldn't drink it."

Dr Olds: "Well, why won't you drink it?"
Patient: "Don't like it."
Dr Olds: "Ever taste it?"
Patient: "Nope."

As transportation and finances improved, the Hospital bought more and more of its food from wholesalers. The garden was let go to weeds, and the barn and root cellars were torn down.

Orange juice became available, yet some patients still wouldn't touch it. Said one, "I don't like orange juice—but I can take that bloomin [albumen] water you gave me."

Long after the Hospital stopped producing its own food, people would bring in a special treat, a few bottles of bakeapple [cloudberry] jam in August perhaps, a few gallons of partridge-berries [mountain cranberry] in September, a mess of seabirds in November month, some seal flippers in March. These the cook would prepare in the good old ways. Even so, homesick patients would find fault.

> **Doctor:** "Skipper, how was your turr? [murre; a local seabird]"
> **Patient:** "The turr was tough, Sir."
> **Doctor:** "Tough?"
> **Patient:** "Well, we could chew the gravy, 'cause we 'ad some mutton 'long with it." Perhaps it is impossible for a hospital kitchen to do justice to turr.

Another delicacy was brook trout. Surely no one could object to wild trout? And yet:

> **Dr Olds:** "Well, Mrs _____, how did you like the trout we served for supper?"
> **Patient:** "Well. . . ."
> **Dr Olds:** "Well what?"
> **Patient:** "Well, Sir, those trouts was so small, it took fourteen or fifteen to make a dozen."

Afterword

John Sheldon, M. D.
New World Island Clinic,
Summerford, Newfoundland *

SAUNDERS '78

I think the greatest change in medicine on these islands is that no longer do we feel self-sufficient, that we should do everything the patient needs. Our place in the world of Newfoundland medicine has changed dramatically. No longer are we a referral centre to which people come from all corners of the province; now we send our patients *to* all corners of the province. Really, we have changed places. We refer our patients to other specialists, to tertiary centres where the high intensity medical care is given.

So a large part of our work now is in attempting to recognize significant disease at an early stage for referral, primarily to St John's but also to Gander and Grand Falls, for their workups and diagnoses and quite often their surgical treatments, unless of course the need for surgery is fairly self-evident.

---

* Author's Note: The above conversation took place in 1989. Major surgery ended at Twillingate in June 1994. No one expected this to happen so soon.

For what these days is considered a cottage hospital, Twillingate probably has more experienced physicians than any other comparable hospital in the province. But I think we all recognize our limitations. We no longer have the necessary backup, in terms of pathology and medical specialists, in the event of complications. So now we tend to do only the straight-forward surgery here.

The pattern of ailments has changed as well. There used to be a lot of tuberculosis. I haven't seen a case on this island for fifteen years now. And the cases one does hear about are mostly patients who had TB in their youth and who in old age suffer a reactivation while seriously ill with another chronic ailment. It's nearly always in the lungs. As well, in the early years one would occasionally see children with tuberculous meningitis or mesenteric adenitis, a form which caused the abdomen to swell up. That's rare now.

Instead—and this is probably typical of most rural areas in Newfoundland—we get a lot of hypertension. And quite a lot of angina, which now often leads to referral and surgery. And there's a lot of diabetes, probably more than in the fifties; one has to suspect increased affluence, plus the change in eating habits.

And there's a lot of chronic anxiety and a good amount of depressive illness.

Not much, however, in the way of serious infectious diseases. And I'm sure less in the way of chronic back strains, which formed a large part of Dr Olds's work. People are much more careful how they work.

It's very striking, actually, in this community, how seldom now we actually suture patients for lacerations. Twenty years ago, we did that every day, often several times a day. Those were mostly axe wounds and cuts from glass lying around on the beaches and on the roads. And chain saw wounds. All relatively uncommon now.

Likewise, car accident cases aren't very common, nor are they generally very serious—though we have had two fatalities here that I can recall.

That's about it. Not many drownings and things like that—touch wood. Everybody's more careful. A different era altogether.

Nobody really told me this when I first came here, but the cross which the hospital doctors really bore back then was that of travelling around the islands. Because often when they got to a place, they'd end up getting called to everybody in the community and spending the day there. I inherited that.

For instance, I was expected to do a clinic in Herring Neck every week. A very primitive affair had been set up in the old post office building. After a short while, I stopped doing it. But Herring Neck had two very forceful directors on the Hospital Board, namely Skipper Joe White, who ran one of Herring Neck's two stores, and Morley Parsons, who ran the other. They were quick to point out that Herring Neck people paid $3 more into their medical plan than did Twillingaters and they damn well wanted their money's worth!

Well, instead of doing the clinic, I went to the houses and visited the people. I remember saying to my wife that a visit to Herring Neck was like going to examine the tentacle of a sick octopus. It was much the same with other communities scattered around New World Island.

However, for me, working in the shadow of a great physician like Dr Olds, it meant that however difficult my medical life became, there was no way I could complain. For I was practising with a doctor who had been through much more than I would ever see.

— J.S.